Partick
Anecdotes

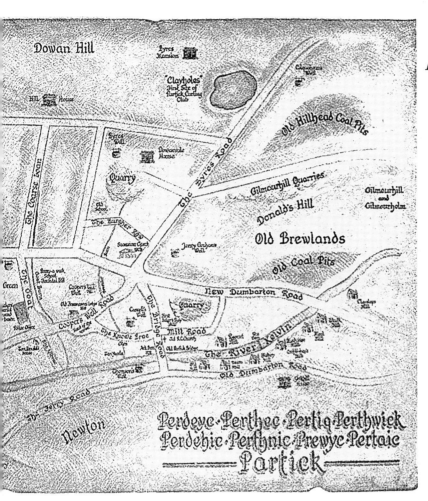

Dowan Hill

Eyres Mansion

"Clayholes"
First Site of
Partick Curling
Club

Hill House

Closeburn Well

Old Hillhead Coal Pits

Eyres Well

Dovecotvale House

The Byres Road

Quarry

Gilmourhill Quarries

Gilmourhill
and
Gilmourholm

Donald's Hill

The Byoker Row

Old Brewlands

Jenny Geohoe's Well

Succession Church

The Goose Loan

Old Coal Pits

New Dumbarton Road

Jenny o'uck School and Sabbath Hill

Cooper's Loan Plot

Green

The Dog Loan

Quarry

Clayhaps Well

Old Insurance Lodge Site

Coxall's Well

Cooper's Well Road

The Bridge Road

Mill Road
old R.C.Church

The Knoke Brae

Pointhouse

Ashton Hill

Old Parish Kirk

The River Kelvin

Old Dumbarton Road

The Ferry Road

Newton

Perdeye · Perthec · Pertiq · Perthwick
Perdehic · Perthnic · Prewyc · Pertaic
— Partick —

Partick
Anecdotes

Compiled

by

Robert M. Paul

First published 1998
by
Jessie Paul and Elizabeth Greer
19 Suffolk Street
Helensburgh
G84 9PA

ISBN 0 9534716 0 8

Printed by
Reproprint Ltd.
Glasgow

Contents

Partick Coat of Arms

ARMORIAL BEARINGS
of the
BURGH OF PARTICK.

In the 1800s, Partick expanded from village to town. It became a Burgh in 1852 but it was not until 1870 that it was decided to have a Coat of Arms. A design was prepared and submitted to the Lord Lyon King at Arms. This was approved in 1872.

The Coat of Arms had a quarterly design. The first and fourth quarters contained a lymphad or one masted galley with oars in action. The second was a castle with two circular towers, argent and sable and the third a Bishop's mitre. The Coat of Arms also contained two millstones and a wheat sheaf.

The castle and the Bishop's mitre commemorate Partick Castle and the Bishops Palace. The millstones and the wheat sheaf are reminders that Partick was at one time a farming area and that there were many mills on the lower Kelvin. The Roman occupation of Yorkhill and the use of the Clyde as a waterway probably inspired the galleys.

The motto "Industria Ditat" – "We are enriched by industry (work)" was rather prophetic as the work of the local community certainly did bring prosperity to Partick.

Partick Customs

The Drum

In Partick, as in many Scottish towns and villages in the sixteenth and seventeenth centuries, it was a common practice for a drummer to parade around the community. He would stop at certain places, beat the Drum, and in a loud voice make public announcements.

The drummer made two tours each day at 5 a.m. and at 9 p.m. In addition, he was in demand on public occasions such as leading the march of Partick Saint Mary's Masonic Lodge and at the election of the office-bearers of the Partick Ploughmen's Friendly Society.

The drummer was elected by a vote at a public meeting and at New Year he received an honorarium by subscription collected from the villagers. His earnings were further increased by the payment for private announcements. These started at 6d per announcement but, as the village grew larger, became 9d and later 11d. In bad weather, he used a tin trumpet instead of a Drum and he was provided with a cloak.

The morning calls ceased about 1820 and the evening calls about 1845, private intimations continued until 1855.

The Funeral Bell

In Partick, as in many Scottish towns and villages, funeral intimations were made by a bell-ringer who stopped at appropriate places and announced details of a funeral. The Partick Funeral Bell bears the date 1726 and was used in this way until 1779.

The Bell disappeared from Partick late in the eighteenth century. It is believed that it was placed in the care of Allan Craig, a local landowner. On his death, his belongings, probably including the Bell, were taken to the home of his son in Edinburgh. It later came into the possession of an Edinburgh sea captain and on his death was purchased by a broker in the Bridgegate of Glasgow. After being sold to a Paisley man, the Bell was purchased by a Mr Ross of Sandyford.

In 1859, Mr Ross returned the Bell to Partick by presenting it to the Partick Curling Club as a trophy. In the Deed of Gift Mr Ross stated that the Bell should not be moved out of Partick farther east than his house in Sandyford. In addition, should the membership of the club become less than eight then the Bell should become the property of the Magistrates and Commissioners of the Burgh of Partick.

Partick's Castles

Partick had three buildings worthy of the title castle – the Castle of the Kings of Strathclyde, the Castle or Palace of the Bishops of Glasgow and a building erected in 1611 which was known locally as the "Castle."

The Castle of the Kings of Strathclyde

The Kingdom of Strathclyde extended northwards from the Solway Firth to the River Forth and westwards to beyond Loch Lomond. The capital was Alcluyd, which was a rocky height on the River Clyde. This was known later as Dumbritton, the Fort of the Britons, which eventually became Dumbarton.

In the "Life of St. Kentigern" written in 1180 by Jocelyn, a monk from Lancashire, it is recorded that Rhydderch or Roderic, King of Strathclyde died in his residence in Partick in 603. Dr Renwick in his "History of Glasgow" confirms this and states that Partick was a "villa regia" – a royal town. The royal residence in Partick could have been a hunting lodge with the hunting taking place on the hilly ground from Gilmorehill to Drumchapel. A suggested site for the lodge is on the right bank of the River Kelvin near its confluence with the Clyde.

The Bishop's Castle

There is evidence of the existence of a Bishop's Castle or Manor at a place called Partick although it is not clear whether this is the same location as the Partick of today.

In 1136, when the Cathedral was dedicated, King David gave to the See of Glasgow some land in Partick, which was tenanted by the Archbishop of Glasgow. This included a manor, which became the residence of the Bishop. A mill was also built on this land. Other proof that there was a Bishop's residence in Partick exists in a deed of 1277 by which timber was purchased from Maurice, Lord of Luss, to repair a bell tower of the Cathedral. This deed has the official seal and was signed at Perthic (Partick). In 1362 certain differences arose between the Bishop of Glasgow and his Chapter and were referred to arbitration at a conference of the Bishops of Scotland. This reference is dated 30th June 1362 and was signed at the Bishop's Mansion, Partick.

It would appear that the Bishops did have a residence in present day Partick at the time of the Reformation in 1560. It is on record that James Beaton, the Archbishop of Glasgow at the Reformation collected several treasures from the Cathedral such as records, writs, charters, crucifixes, chalices, and candlesticks and secreted them in the Meal Mill of Partick before taking them to France. The Bishop's residence in Partick was in all probability a summer residence.

Partick "Castle"

Partick "Castle" was the title given by local people to a building on the site of the Bishop's Manor. It could be that the stone of the manor was used in its construction. The castle was situated to the south of Castlebank Street opposite Anderson Street. It was built in 1611 for George Hutcheson, one of the Hutcheson brothers, who founded the Hutcheson Trust and Hutcheson's Grammar School. The builder was William Wilson from Kilwinning who brought his own workmen and who introduced freemasonry to Partick.

By 1775, the castle was a complete ruin, its stone being used for building elsewhere in Partick. The stone was probably used in the construction of the Merklands farmhouse, which is to the right of the castle.

The Bridges of Partick

The "Old Bridge."

This bridge, shown in an 1846 watercolour, spanned the Kelvin from the foot of Bridge Street on one side of the river to the foot of Yorkhill on the other.

There may have been an earlier bridge. Tradition has it that a wooden footbridge existed above the Archbishop's Mill. There were also several fords.

It is estimated that the "Old Bridge" was built between 1570 and 1601. It may well have been built shortly after the Regent Moray gifted the Archbishop's Mill to the Incorporation of Bakers in 1568. What is certain is that Captain Crawford of Jordanhill repaired the Bridge in 1601 and may have added an arch at that time. When the bridge was built, it was only wide

enough to take one cart, however, in 1800 it was widened to take two carts.

The bridge was demolished in September 1895 and two sculpted slabs were preserved. One slab had the Crawford Arms with the date 1601, and the other marked L.S.D.L., Ludovic Stewart, and Duke of Lennox, had the Lennox Arms and the same date.

The "Old Bridge" – view towards Partick Cross

The sentry type box in the foreground is for the toll collector. Tolls were collected for animals and carts crossing the bridge especially at Fair times, such as the Dumbarton Fair in June and the Balloch Fair in September. The church on the right is St Simon's.

The Kelvin at Partick Bridge circa 1780

These houses with thatched roofs and crow-stepped gables were on the north bank of the Kelvin at the "Old Bridge," about 200 yards south of the present Partick Cross. One of the arches of the bridge can be seen on the right. In the eighteenth century, Partick's domestic water supply was obtained from the burns and various wells scattered throughout the village – hence the woman drawing water from the Kelvin.

Dumbarton Road Bridge

By the end of the eighteenth century, the "Old Bridge", despite having been widened, was becoming inadequate to cope with the increase in traffic, and a stronger bridge was needed.

In the records of the Burgh of Glasgow, it is stated that on the 10th August 1797 the Magistrates gave £100 towards the cost of building a new bridge and changing the course of the main road from Glasgow to Dumbarton.

At that time New Dumbarton Road, later Argyle Street, had been improved as far as Overnewton. From Overnewton, the road went westward along Old Dumbarton Road (behind the Kelvin Hall), across the Kelvin by the "Old Bridge" then followed the line of the present Dumbarton Road. It was realised

that a much more direct route westwards could be taken by having a fork at Overnewton, improving the road to the right, and crossing the Kelvin much higher up the river. The road would then run directly to the foot of present day Church Street and then swing round to Partick Cross.

The new bridge was a stone structure with three arches over the river and a smaller arch over the lade to the Bunhouse Mill. The bridge is now located within the grounds of Kelvingrove Park.

Note the gates on the side of the bridge. These gates facilitate the disposal of snow and ice cleared from the streets in winter. There are similar gates for the same purpose on the Clyde at Meadowside and on the Kelvin at Kelvinbridge.

Partick Bridge

Partick Bridge and Art Galleries.

By 1870, the growing shipbuilding industry in Partick had resulted in a great increase of traffic into the district. Owing to this increase in traffic and particularly the increase in the weight of the vehicles; the existing bridge was showing signs of strain. The arches were displaying slight displacement and the approach roads were showing some subsidence. The Glasgow and Yoker Turnpike Trust, who owned the road and the bridge, resolved to build a new bridge capable of taking two tramlines, horse drawn trams having been introduced in 1872. In 1876, Bell and Miller were appointed engineers and Hugh Kennedy and Company was appointed as contractor.

The foundation stone to the bridge was laid in 1877 by Hugh Kirkwood of Killermont and is sandstone from Wemyss Bay. Hugh Kennedy was Provost of Partick from 1878-1883 and his firm was involved in cutting the railway from Greenock to Wemyss Bay. Much of the red sandstone excavated was used for building purposes and examples in Partick are the red sandstone houses on the west side of Merkland Street and the houses in Sauchiehall Street overlooking Kelvingrove Park. Hugh Kennedy's son William was Provost from 1902-1905.

A direct route was taken from the Bunhouse Football Park – on the east side of Bunhouse Road and now part of the Kelvin Hall – and a new road was constructed. The old road became a roadway in the park. The bridge, which was originally known as Kelvin Bridge, is a skew-arched bridge with nine ribs. The spaces between the outer girders have gothic tracery. At the east end of the span is the Coat of Arms of Glasgow and at the west end the Arms of Partick.

William Collins, the Lord Provost of Glasgow, opened the bridge in 1878.

Benalder Street Bridge

This photograph shows Partick Central Station, later the Kelvin Hall Railway Station, which closed in 1965. Both the railway and the station were built for the Lanarkshire and Dunbartonshire Railway Company in 1896. The railway ran along the north bank of the Kelvin and cut off access to the "Old Bridge." To compensate, the railway company constructed a new iron bridge. The bridge consisted of a single span, open lattice type girder over the Kelvin with four shorter spans over the railway.

The station had the booking office at bridge level and stairs leading down to the platforms. The platforms were built on what at one time was a very productive orchard. The alluvial soil of the lower Kelvin was particularly fertile.

The Waterside of Partick

Stepping Stones Across the Kelvin

An important right-of-way in the village of Partick was the Steps Road leading to the Stepping-Stones. This was the easiest way to travel from Partick to Govan. The Steps Road led from Castlebank Street at the foot of present day Anderson Street to the Stepping-Stones across the Kelvin. It then followed a path along the east bank of the river to the Clyde ferry at Pointhouse.

The owner of the slit mill, to the left of the picture, was not happy with people using this right-of-way. In winter, the stones were frequently displaced by flood and he objected to stones from his land being used for repair purposes.

In the middle of the last century the steps were badly in need of repair and it was proposed that a bridge be erected. Wilson of the slit mill was strongly opposed to the project. Legal advice was sought on the right of the local people to build a bridge and the opinion was in their favour. A subscription list was opened and the bridge was completed in 1863. The opening was a great occasion with the village band turning out and the villagers marching in a procession to the bridge.

Unfortunately, winter floods swept the bridge downstream and the problem of crossing the river remained. In 1865, there was an agreement with Messrs A. & J. Inglis of Pointhouse Shipyard whereby the villagers would give up their right-of-way in return for a bridge being built. This new bridge was swept away in December 1876 and was not replaced.

When the North British Railway Company built a bridge across the Kelvin in 1873 an arrangement between Partick Town Council, A. & J. Inglis and the Railway Company resulted in a pathway being built along the Railway Bridge. This became known to the locals as the "Iron Bridge". Access to the bridge was down Anderson Street, across Castlebank Street, along the Otter Lane then up a flight of stairs to the bridge. After crossing the bridge there was another flight of steps to Pointhouse Ferry Road and along to the ferry. This route was used at night to reach the 24-hour passenger ferry. With the building of the Clydeside Expressway in 1973, the Railway Bridge, along with its pathway, was demolished.

Pointhouse Crossing

This painting by William Simpson dated 1845 shows the Pointhouse Crossing between Partick and Govan.

There has been a river crossing at Pointhouse for several centuries. It is probable that the Romans used it on their journeys between their main camp on the Gleniffer Braes and the outpost station at Yorkhill. In 1755, John Smeaton, a consultant engineer from Leeds, was commissioned to prepare a scheme for deepening the River Clyde. He carried out surveys of the shallow places on the river and found that at low tide the depth of the water at Pointhouse was a mere 15 inches. At that time, even at high tide,

the crossing was easily fordable by horse-drawn vehicles.

By the late eighteenth century, the Smithfield Iron Company who owned the Slit Mill on the Kelvin operated a ferry across the Clyde. In 1781, Smithfield put the mill, the land it stood on, and the ferry at Pointhouse on the market.

The painting shows an early vehicular ferry, which was operated by a chain fixed to both banks, which passed over a cogwheel. The rotation of the cog by the ferry crew drew the boat from one side to the other. The spire of Govan Parish Church and boatmen fishing for salmon can also be seen.

Pointhouse Ferry

The River Trustees purchased the first elevating ferry at Pointhouse in 1912. This ferry was withdrawn in 1938 when Fleming and Ferguson of Paisley built the elevating ferry shown in the photograph.

The platform, for the vehicles and passengers, was suspended from high girders and could be raised and lowered by winches to be level with the landing stage no matter the height of the tide. The ferry was of the double-ended type and had propellers, so there was no need to turn.

The ferry's duties were not always mundane. During an air raid on 18th September 1940 a 250lbs bomb hit a cruiser HMS Sussex in Yorkhill basin. It penetrated all three decks and lay, unexploded, on the platform deck deep in the ship. The ship was on fire and the chance of the ship's magazines, which were fully loaded, being detonated, was high. Fire fighting equipment was taken aboard the ferry and it was steered alongside the stricken vessel to extinguish the fire. A potentially massive and terrible explosion was avoided.

With the opening of the Clyde Tunnel in 1965 the vehicular ferry at Pointhouse was withdrawn and later sold to an oil company.

To the left of the vehicular ferry can be seen the berth occupied by the passenger ferry. The passenger ferry was introduced at the beginning of the century and operated both day and night. The passenger ferry closed a year after the vehicular ferry.

Meadowside Passenger Ferry

This was the passenger ferry, which ran between Partick and Govan. The service was run by the Clyde Navigation Trust and operated between Meadowside Street in Partick and Wanlock Street (formerly Holm Street) in Govan. The fare was collected at a turnstile on the Partick side but this was discontinued in 1920 when the Clyde Navigation Trust was subsidised by Glasgow Corporation. For a time, after the fares ceased, the ferry was besieged by youths crossing and recrossing the river.

When the shipyards were busy traffic was very heavy and at rush hours, there were long queues for the ferry. At these times, an additional ferry was brought into service. This double service also ran on Saturday afternoons when Rangers were playing at Ibrox.

The ferry service ended on 22nd January 1966.

Partick Pier

The construction of a pier at Partick was greatly accelerated by an accident on the 6th April 1861.

Workers from Robert Napier's shipyard, who lived in Partick, were travelling home from Greenock on the steamer Lochneil. It was Saturday night and many of the workers had been drinking. There was no pier at Partick and the Govan ferry, which was a rowing boat for 24 passengers, acted as a tender. When it came alongside the Lochneil so many of the passengers scrambled aboard that the boat sank. Despite the rescue efforts of the Captain and his crew, six of the workers were drowned. As a result of this tragedy, work was started on a pier at Partick.

Partick Pier was at the foot of Pointhouse Road about 100 yards east of the mouth of the River Kelvin. It was closed on November 1906 when the last steamer was the Lochgoil steamer, the Edinburgh Castle. In the photograph, taken early this century, the steamer is the Caledonia.

In his reminiscences of the Victorian gentry, "I Remember" published in 1932; J.J. Bell, creator of "Wee McGregor", gives an interesting account of travel from Partick Pier. He recalls that Partick Pier was used by the "well to do" residents of the west end of Glasgow for their trips down the river.

Meadowside Graving Dock

There is no evidence of shipbuilding at Partick prior to 1821 when T.B. Seath opened a shipyard at Meadowside on the site of a printwork and bleachfield. In 1844 Seath's shipyard was taken over by Messrs Tod and McGregor who had operated previously on the south bank of the river.

The area lacked a graving dock and it was left to Tod and McGregor (later D & W Henderson Ltd) of Meadowside Shipyard to finance its construction.

The dock was built on land between the shipyard and the River Kelvin and was designed by Bell and Miller. Construction began in 1856 and the graving dock was opened on 28th January 1858.

It was a massive undertaking and was a world leader in its day. About 320,000 cartloads of earth were dug out to create the cavity for the dock. Over 7,000 cartloads of cement were needed for the foundations and over 500,000 cubic feet of stone were used for the walls, which were 23 feet thick at the base. The dock's iron gates weighed 70 tons. The surface area of the dock was one acre and 1,200 feet of wharfage was built along the Kelvin. The dock could be pumped dry in two hours.

It was used for shipbuilding and repair during the Second World War. In 1969 it was filled in and became a parking area for haulage contractors.

Meadowside Granary

It had long been recognised that the stretch of the river from Merklands to Yorkhill could be redeveloped as additional berthage. In 1907, the River Trustees purchased the ground to build a quay. Partick Thistle F.C. owned much of the ground and only when arrangements were finalised to relocate the club to Maryhill could construction work on the 572 yard long Meadowside Quay begin.

In 1914, the Meadowside Granary was completed on the ground behind the quay. It was a small dark brick building but in 1935, the first extension was built and the new silos could store an additional 15,000 tons of grain. This is the brick section on the right of the photograph. The second extension was built in 1960 and is the large structure to the left. It had a capacity of 50,000 tons and to increase the rate of ship unloading six new 200 tons per hour suction elevators were built. Another building was erected in 1966 with a capacity of 80,000 tons.

The 1914 and the 1936 buildings are now closed and the 1960 and 1966 buildings used for the storage of maize, barley and wheat. At present, the grain is brought in by road.

Milling in Partick

For well over four hundred years, the waters of the Kelvin have provided the power for driving mills. On the stretch between Kelvindale and where the Kelvin flows into the Clyde there have been paper mills, flint mills, snuff mills, wheat mills, barley mills, and slit mills.

Bishop Mill

The mill in the photograph was on the site of the Bishop Mill – known also as the Mill of Partick. It is beside the "Old Bridge" and is the oldest recorded mill site in the district. The original mill, said to have been built in 1136, was given in 1571 to Captain Crawford of Jordanhill by the Bishop of Glasgow as a reward for storming Dumbarton Castle. The Bishop, however, persuaded Captain Crawford to return the mill to the Church in 1599 and it later became town property. The mill was burned down in 1836 and a new mill was built in 1839 and enlarged in 1855.

Bishop Mill was a four-storey construction of coarse rubble, which had wheat sheaves at the apices of the gables. It was powered by a water wheel and until the 1950s by a turbine, when in turn steam, gas, petrol and latterly electricity provided the power. It was owned for many years by the White family and was a busy mill employing around a dozen workers producing pulses and cattle fodder. It ceased production in the early 1970s.

After the mill was closed, the future of the building was uncertain for some time. Finally, it was bought by a property company, Regency Properties Ltd. The exterior of the building was retained and the interior converted to apartments and the development named Bishop Mill Court.

Regent and Scotstoun Mills

Two mills, which continued into the twentieth century, were the Regent Mill and Scotstoun Mill.

The Regent Mill, on the left of the photograph, was built on the site of the Archbishop's Mill. On one side of its foundation stone it is recounted how the mill was a gift from Regent Moray to the Incorporation of Bakers in Glasgow as a reward for supplying his forces with bread during the 1568 campaign which culminated in the Battle of Langside. At this time, the mill was known as the Bunhouse Mill. In 1652, the Incorporation of Bakers rebuilt the mill. It was further enlarged in 1828 and operated successfully until it was destroyed by fire in 1886.

On the other side of the foundation stone is a list of the office-bearers of the Incorporation. The foundation stone was uncovered at the time of the fire.

The shell of the building was purchased by Mr John Ure, a former Deacon of the Incorporation of Bakers and an ex Lord Provost of the City of Glasgow. He sold the mill to the Scottish Co-operative Wholesale Society in 1903. It was fitted with the latest machinery and its main product was "Lofty Peak" flour. It was renamed the Regent Mill and was very successful until the late 1970s when milling activities were moved to Chancelot Mill at Leith docks. Eventually the building was demolished and in its place, there is now a car park.

The Scotstoun Mill in Partick Bridge Street occupies the site of the Waulk Mill, which was built in 1507 for the preparation of woollen cloth. From the late eighteenth century it was in the possession of the Scotstoun family. In 1834 it was sold to a Mr John White and was operated as a flour and grain mill. The White Family was a highly respected Partick Family. Mr John White was Provost of Partick from 1857-1860; his son also John was Provost from 1905-1908. In 1933 the Scotstoun Mill was acquired by Spillers Ltd.

The present building was erected in 1877. It is now known as the Glasgow Mill and is owned by Rank Hovis Ltd.

By the favour of Almighty God.
This Compartment or Division of the Mills of
Partick, belonging to
The Incorporation of Bakers in Glasgow,
Being now to be rebuilt on the Site of
The "Ancient Quheite Mill of Partick,"
Donated in the Year 1568
by
His Highness, James, Earl of Moray, Regent
of Scotland, to
The Bakers of Glasgow,
In reward for their Zeal in the cause of the
Protestant Reformation, and
For their spirited and well-timed assistance to
him and his Forces
At the eventful and decisive Battle of Langside,
This foundation stone was laid by
William Smith, Esq., late Lord Provost of
Glasgow,
And a Member of this Incorporation,
On the 23rd day of May,
Anno Domini 1828,
In the ninth year of the Reign of our
Most Gracious Sovereign,
George The Fourth,
In presence of the Deacon, Collector, Master
Court, and Building Committee,
And also in presence of
A number of the other Members of the
Incorporation;
Which undertaking
May the Supreme God
Bless and Prosper.

Local Services

Partick Pumping Station

Before 1894, the domestic and business sewage of both Glasgow and the Clyde Valley was discharged into the Clyde without any treatment. There was comparatively little danger to public health as long as the river could provide the necessary dilution. This became harder as the population of Glasgow mushroomed from 77,000 in 1801 to around 650,000 in 1891. The stretch of the river between Bridgeton and Clydebank took the brunt of the pollution.

In 1896, special powers were obtained to proceed with improvements in the drainage from the western part of Glasgow including Partick, Clydebank, and parts of Dunbartonshire. Sewage Disposal Works were built at Dalmuir and a large intermediate pumping station was built at Partick. Both started operating in 1904. The sludge from the works was disposed of in the Firth of Clyde between Garroch Head and Arran. For many years, the carriers were the steamers "Shieldhall" and the "Dalmarnock". Both had a capacity of about 1,500 tons of sludge. Their successors were larger and the sludge continued to be dumped off Arran. E.EC. legislation deemed that this practise had to cease on 31st December 1998.

The Partick pumping station is an ornate, renaissance, red sandstone building on the west bank of the Kelvin in Dumbarton Road. It deals with low level drainage from the Saltmarket to Scotstoun. Originally, the pumping plant comprised of 3 steam driven triple expansion pumps but these were replaced in 1961 by electric pumps. The photograph shows the chimney used when there were coal fired boilers. The chimney was demolished in February 1988.

Horse Tramway Stables

This building is in Thurso Street (formerly Queen Street) on the south side of Dumbarton Road opposite Church Street. It was built in 1883 for the Glasgow Tramway and Omnibus Company as stables for the horses and sheds for the vehicles. The sheds were on the ground floor, the stables on the first floor and the attic housed the animal fodder. Two hundred and forty horses could be stabled and thirty vehicles garaged.

The top floors were removed, additional floors built, and for many years, the building was used as a grain store. More recently, Glasgow University has occupied it as a garage, workshops, and the Glasgow University Business Archive.

The outline of a gable of a former adjoining building can be seen to the left of the old stable building. This was a tenement built for the tramway workers. The conditions of employment for these men were considered good. They earned 27 shillings a week and their working day lasted about 14.5 hours. They also had the benefit of their work being permanent unlike so many of the time who suffered hardship owing to the seasonal or cyclical nature of their work.

Early Partick Buses

Wylie and Lochhead ran the first bus service between Partick and Glasgow using an old fashioned stagecoach. By 1844, it was replaced by an omnibus. A service ran every two or three hours with a single fare of four pence. The original stable was at the foot of Crow Road. In 1850, a stable was obtained in Whiteinch, and a regular service with two buses was provided. Wylie and Lochhead withdrew their service in 1860 when six Partick businessmen started up the Glasgow and Partick Omnibus Company.

In 1847, a Mr James Walker ("Hookey" Walker) began a service between Partick and Glasgow. Eventually he had two services. The first was via Finnieston and Anderston to the centre of the city. The second was from Downhill to the Royal Exchange.

"Hookey" Walker also introduced a Sunday service for those who lived in Partick but went to church in Glasgow. This caused serious disquiet at the time and The Argus, a Glasgow newspaper, reported "sensational event in Partick – proposal to run a Sabbath bus." The solution was to sell tickets on Saturday and not to pick up anyone *en route*.

The Glasgow and Partick Omnibus Company had stables in Whiteinch on the south side of Dumbarton Road about a quarter of a mile west of the present Clyde Tunnel entrance. Their buses ran from these stables to the foot of Queen Street in Glasgow.

There was great rivalry between these early bus companies. The buses were painted in distinctive colours. Wylie and Lochhead's were blue; Walker's were brown and the Partick and Glasgow Omnibus Company green. The competition was very keen as they raced each other to the first stage. The journey across the narrow Partick Bridge could be hair-raising for the passengers.

A contemporary poem highlights the situation:

On Partick road when fares were high,
The Buses slow and patrons shy,
Then "Walker," "Wylie" was the cry,
Round Kelvin rolling leisurely.

But Partick saw another sight,
When the green bus began the fight,
Demanding with all Partick's might,
That hours and fares be limited.

The bus in the picture is a green three horse Glasgow and Partick Omnibus Company bus at the Whiteinch stables around 1860.

Horse Drawn Ambulance

This photograph was taken at the entrance to Knightswood Hospital at the beginning of this century. The Ambulance was used mostly for infectious diseases and was known as the "Fever Van." Mothers often threatened their unruly children to send them away in the "Fever Van."

Early Motor Ambulance

This is the first motor ambulance of Knightswood Hospital and the photograph was taken when the vehicle was delivered to the Hospital Board who can be seen at the front of the ambulance.

The ambulance spare wheel is interesting. It is a Stepney Spare Wheel and if a puncture occurred the affected wheel was fixed to the hub by a special attachment and the vehicle proceeded on five wheels.

First Partick Police Office

The building was in Castlebank Street at the west corner of Kelvin Street (now Keith Street) and just south of the Quakers' Burial Ground. The barrow seen outside the door was used on Friday and Saturday evenings to transport inebriates to the cells.

Despite an increase in population, there was no local policing in Partick until 1844 when a committee was formed to supervise the appointment of a policeman. The need for change was highlighted in 1843 when a drunken group of Irish labourers started a riot in Partick and application had to be made to the Sheriff in Glasgow to restore order. He did so and for a time, the Anderston Police patrolled Partick. It was then agreed that the men of the village should act as watchmen to retain the peace. They soon tired of this obligation and Andrew Gibson was employed as the first village policeman.

The "Marine" Police Office

Because of the demands for an increased police service in Partick, a new building was constructed in 1872 in Anderson Street. The tenement beyond the main building was built to provide houses for the police but this was subsequently incorporated into the main police station. The low building to the left was the cellblock with thirty cells. The "Marine" also contained a fair sized court.

A major incident occurred on 5th August 1875 when a procession passing through the village in honour of the O'Connel Celebrations deteriorated into a riot. The Riot Act was read and the Glasgow Police were summoned. Special Constables were also enrolled. Unrest lasted for a number of days and the court was kept busy for

several days. This episode became known as the "Partick Riots."

By 1888, the Partick force had grown to 53 and in 1901 it had grown further to 77. In 1912, at the time of the annexation with Glasgow, the force had a chief constable, two inspectors, three detectives, and eighty-seven constables. On annexation, the Partick Force was called the Partick Division and in 1931, it became "B" Division. It was also known as the "Marine" Division because the River Police were based at Partick.

The "Marine" was closed in 1993 and has been converted into a Centre for Sensory Impairment. A new Police Office was opened in Thornwood on the site of Partick West Station.

Partick Fire Station

In the 1870s, the Partick Fire Service was a force of five firemen. By the time of the annexation, it had grown to a full-time professional force of a firemaster, a deputy firemaster, and ten firemen.

The first fire station was in Wilson Street, now Gullane Street, near the police office. In the event of a fire, the police summoned the firemen from home or work by ringing a bell from the roof of the police station. In 1893, the fire station moved to Anderson Street.

This fire station became inadequate for the needs of the expanding burgh and a new station was built in Hozier Street (Beith Street). The picture shows the opening ceremony on 21st May 1907. Mrs John White wife of Provost White opened

the station. In 1914, an extension was built to provide additional houses for the staff.

The station was closed in 1985 and the building was bought by the Meadowside and Thornwood Housing Association and converted into 23 flats.

Early Motor Fire Engine

This vehicle was delivered to the Partick Fire Service in 1912. It was built by the Halley Company of Yoker and was a highly sophisticated piece of apparatus for its day as it was able to pump 500 gallons of water per minute. After the annexation, the vehicle was stationed at Ingram Street Fire Station in the centre of the city. The people of Partick were extremely unhappy at this move and the appliance was eventually returned to Partick.

Partick Baths and Washhouse

Towards the end of last century, some councillors felt that the community should be provided with a municipal Baths and Washhouse. The locals did not seem to share their councillors' enthusiasm and the matter was not pursued.

The population was housed in tenements with a wash house in the backcourt of each close. Each house was allocated a time to use the wash house. On wash day, the boiler had to be lit early in the morning to ensure a supply of hot water. It was not uncommon to employ a washerwoman for the day. By the turn of the century, the need for a commercial washhouse became more acceptable and in June 1912 on the eve of annexation, it was agreed that a Baths and Washhouse should be built. The ground from Walker Street to Dumbarton Road was reserved by the Burgh for municipal buildings. The Baths and Washhouse was built in Douglas Street (Purdon Street) at the corner with Walker Street near Partick Library. Baillie Sloan opened the building on 26th January 1914. The total cost was £9,000.

The gap between the Library and the Baths and Washhouse was intended for Swimming Baths but after the annexation, these never materialised. For long, this was a "sore" point in Partick.

In the early 1960s, the Baths and Washhouse underwent extensive modernisation and it became the Partick Launderette. With changing lifestyles, Partick Launderette finally closed in 1996.

Partick Burgh Hall

The Burgh Hall was built in 1872 in Maxwell now Burgh Hall Street. It was designed by the celebrated Glasgow architect William Leiper who also designed Dowanhill Church. The sculpture work was by John Young. Both the Burgh Hall and Dowanhill Church are currently "B" listed buildings.

When the hall was built a pipe organ was installed. The cost of the instrument was raised by public subscription. The organ was removed just after the First World War.

In 1912, an extension was built on the immediate east of the building. This included a Lesser Burgh Hall and some additional rooms. Subsequently more accommodation was acquired in buildings extending to Fortrose Street. On the walls of the Lesser Hall were wooden panels with the names and dates of the Provosts of Partick inscribed. These were removed during refurbishment in 1988.

Buildings of Interest

Old Masons' Inn

A member of the Craig family, noted landowners in Partick, built this building in 1619. It was situated on the north side of Castlebank Street a little to the west of the present Keith Street. This site, which became P & R Fleming's assembly yard, has been replaced by a housing development.

For many years, it was the main inn and public house in Partick. At the rear of the building was the brew house for the brewing of ale. It was demolished in 1879 having stood for 260 years.

The inn was the regular meeting place of the Partick Masonic Lodges and led to the name "Masons' Inn." Masonry has been practised in Partick since about 1611 when William Miller, a Glasgow builder was given a contract to build a house in Partick. Miller came from Kilwinning and brought skilled masons who were members of the Craft. He inaugurated a lodge, which operated in Partick without a charter until 1759 when the lodge became Partick Kilwinning No.64.

In 1763, a schism occurred and a breakaway lodge was formed and was granted its charter in 1769. This lodge was named Partick Saint Mary's No.150 later changing to No.117. Partick Kilwinning No.64 was dissolved in 1839 when their lodge was destroyed by fire. Partick Saint Mary's met regularly in the Masons' Inn until 1840. Subsequently it met in various places until the Masonic Halls at 92 Dumbarton Road were purchased.

Byres of Partick

Two hundred years ago the area of Partick north of Partick Cross and rising towards Hillhead was known as the Castle Hill. This name had no connection with Partick Castle but referred to a large mansion house, roughly on the site of the present Athole Gardens.

This hilly area provided grazing for the dairy herds of the Bishop's Palace and there were byres for the cattle – hence Byres Road.

In addition, there was a large house with a small clachan or township of cottages called the "Byres of Partick" one of the cottages is shown in the sketch. It was thought that this cottage was on the west side of Byres Road near present day Lawrence Street.

In the 1860s Byres Road ran from Partick Cross to Lawrence Street. From Lawrence Street to Great Western Road, it was called Victoria Street. It was suggested that the whole roadway be renamed Victoria Road, but this was never adopted.

First Baker's Shop

There was no baker in Partick until 1820 when Alexander Campbell opened his shop in a house in Bridge Street on what is now the site of St. Simon's Church. After a few years, he sold the business to John Wilson who continued successfully for many years. The shop was famed for its mutton pies.

Heid o' the Goat

These buildings were on Dumbarton Road at the corner of Keith Street on the site of the present Comet warehouse. Keith Street was formerly known as Kelvin Street and when Partick was a village, it was known as "The Goat."

"Goat" is an old Scots word meaning "a trench" and was applied to the ditch alongside a road. The "Heid o' the Goat" was a noted place in Partick since it was a favourite rendezvous for men on weekday evenings and on Saturdays where they discussed world problems. In addition, religious speakers, travelling salesmen and entertainers also gathered there.

Tom Burns, a Partick poet of last century wrote an account of the happenings at the "Heid o' the Goat".

A place in oor toon has a gae funny name,
An search Scotland roon ye'll no get ane
    the same,
Though its richt name's in print on a
    prominent spot,
The ane its best kent by the Heid o' the
    Goat.

There tradesman o' every class you will
    find,

In guid Doric language expressing their mind,
Hoo ships should be built, ay an mony a boat,
Has been feenished and lenched at the Heid o' the Goat.

A' kinds o' doctors come wi' their pills,
An feesick that's bound tae cure a sorts o' ills,
For tichake or asthma, the real antidote,
Can only be had at the Heid o' the Goat.

If a wandering acrobat came to oor toon,
The Goat is the place whaur he pits his props doon,
But'less he can tummel an' flip flap a lot,
He'll no mak maik at the Heid o' the Goat.

The man wha sells paste that makes brass shine like gold,

The chap wha sells books whaurin' fortunes are told,
An the chiel wha can sell you a cheap hat or coat
Can be found doing "biz" at the Heid o' the Goat.

The houses in the photograph were built in brick, which probably came from the Jordanhill Brickworks. The doors on the street were like stable doors – a separate upper and lower half. Next to the horse and cart in the photograph can be seen a pend leading to a backyard where there was a joiner's and a plumber's shop. The horse and cart probably belonged to a Mr Miller who ran a coal merchant and removal business. He was well known locally for his success in caring for sick horses. The houses were demolished about 1930.

The Knowe

The Knowe was a group of houses near the banks of the Kelvin on what later became the site of Partick Central Station. A roadway, the Knowe Brae, ran between the houses northward to the Knowe Head, a short street at the foot of the Goat. The Knowe Head, which ran east to west, subsequently became part of Castlebank Street.

Parliament Close

These houses stood in Castlebank Street to the east of the Goat. The houses were demolished in the 1920s. The entrance to the Goat can be seen to the left of the photograph. The opening to the right of the buildings led to weavers' houses and workshops. It was known as Parliament Close where the weavers held open air meetings and debated the affairs of the day. It was the Partick equivalent of Hyde Park Corner.

Yorkhill House

Yorkhill House stood on the east bank of the Kelvin where the Clyde and Kelvin meet. It looked out south towards the Renfrewshire Hills and west down the River Clyde. It was situated in the extreme west of the Overnewton Estate and was built in 1805 for R.F. Alexander, a Glasgow Merchant.

In 1813, the house was sold to Andrew Gilbert a Glasgow Underwriter whose niece became the wife of Sir John Graham, a noted Scottish portrait painter, and art connoisseur. On the death of Mr Gilbert, his niece inherited the property and under the terms of the will John Graham adopted the name Gilbert and became John Graham-Gilbert. He occupied the house until his death in 1866. His widow bequeathed his art collection to the Corporation of the City of Glasgow.

Workmen uncovered a number of Roman remains while preparing a new garden in the grounds of Yorkhill estate. These remains included coins, a large thumb ring, fragments of vessels, and some wheat. The wheat must have been imported because it was not grown in Scotland in Roman times. One of the coins is of particular interest because it bears the image of the Roman Emperor Trajan who ruled from AD 98 until AD 117. It was well preserved although it must have been in the soil for around 1600 years. This could substantiate the claim that Yorkhill was an out-station of the Roman fort at Vandura on the Gleniffer Braes at Paisley.

The house remained in the family after the artist's death and the last occupier was the widow of Mr C.A. Crerer-Gilbert who lived in Yorkhill House until it was bought to be the site of the Royal Hospital for Sick Children. The estate covered 19 acres and cost £16,000. King George V and Queen Mary opened the hospital on the 7th July 1914. It so happened that at the same time Jordanhill Estate came on the market and some argued that Jordanhill should be the site of the hospital and that Yorkhill should be the site of the college for teacher training.

In 1965, a survey of the hospital building revealed serious defects in the steel concrete structure. The staff and the patients were removed in January 1966 to Oakbank Hospital until the replacement was ready in October 1971. In the meantime, the Queen Mother's Maternity Hospital, which opened in 1964, had been built on the former staff playing fields.

Norfolk House

This house was in Purdon (formerly Douglas) Street on the same side as the library just beyond the Baths and Washhouse. John Walker, who owned the bleachfield, which is now the site of housing behind Partick South Church, built the house in the early part of last century.

In the picture taken in the late 1960s, the facade of the original building can be clearly seen, the doorway with windows on each side and the six windows above.

Late last century the building was enlarged and it became a Model Lodging House. Later an extension at the side was built which gave the house capacity for 318 men. Until just after the Second World War Norfolk House was home to many who worked in the shipyards, docks, and the engineering works of Clydeside.

The lodging house was closed around 1950 and the building was taken over by the Glasgow Education Department and used as a store for school furniture. It was closed in the mid 1960s and subsequently demolished.

The street to the north of Norfolk House was called Walker Street and the street to the south was Grace Street after his daughter. The name "Walker" endures in the housing complex close by called Walker Court.

Miss Grace Walker was a very caring person and was very involved with the local community. A small hall with ancillary accommodation was built by Mr Walker in Purdon Street opposite the Washhouse. This was known as "Miss Walker's Working Girls Club." It not only offered the young women of the district recreational activities but also trained them to sew and dress-make along with basic housekeeping and cookery. In addition, the club had a bath for their use, which was something that their own dwellings lacked. The club continued into the 1930s and was later taken over by the Salvation Army.

Granny Gibb's Cottage

"Granny Gibb's Cottage" which was situated in Dumbarton Road near Sawmill Road was built by her husband in 1796. It was an inn and was well patronised by West Highland drovers on their way with cattle and sheep to the market in Glasgow.

"Crow Road" may be derived from the Gaelic "crodh" –"cattle." The line of the present Crow Road would be the route used by the drovers on their way to Partick *en route* to Glasgow. Partick was a favourite stopping place where the animals could be rested and watered so that they would arrive at the market place in good condition. The inns of Partick depended on this trade and consequently Partick had more inns than the population merited. Monday was the market day in Glasgow. So if a drover arrived on a Saturday, Granny Gibb who was a strict Sabbatarian, would not allow him to take his animals from her field at the back of the house until Monday morning.

On the death of her husband, who was a vintner in Partick, Granny Gibb moved to an inn near Partick Cross but after two years she returned to her cottage.

In 1896, the cottage was demolished to make way for tenements at 671 and 673 Dumbarton Road. These dwellings were in turn demolished for the approaches to the roundabout at the foot of Broomhill Drive.

George Boyce, a Partick poet, composed a poem at the time of the death of Granny Gibb.

The first verses are as follows

Old Granny Gibb has passed away,
So has her late abode,
Her wee hoose stood for many a day
A landmark near the road.

Above it's bordering field of green,
The lark sang sweet and loud
When it's wee form was dimly seen,
Amidst the drifting cloud.

With cheerful notes its ear to charm,
The wee bird did its best;
The place we once called Merkland Farm
Is now called Partick West.

The drovers passing east and west,
Knew her wee hoose of call,
With highland whisky called the best
She could supply them all.

The Last Houses of Partick Village

These houses were in Anderson Street opposite Partick Anderson Church which is now part of the present day Safeway car park. They were the last occupied houses of the old village. The houses were well-kept dwellings but lacked modern facilities and were demolished in 1975.

Education in Partick

Subscription School

The first school in Partick was built about 1750 on part of the Common Loan, a broad stretch of open ground, extending roughly from Castlebank Street to the present Chancellor Street. The school was probably under the care and control of the Kirk Session of Govan Parish Church, as each parish church was responsible for the education facilities throughout its parish.

A schoolmaster was appointed to instruct the children in reading, writing, and arithmetic. James Lapsley, an innkeeper in Partick, bequeathed ten pounds to the heritors of Partick for charitable purposes and the heritors declared that the annual interest from this bequest should be paid to the schoolmaster to augment his income.

By 1790, this school had fallen into disrepair and three public-minded men – John Purdon of Bridge End, William Robb of Meadowside, and Allan Craig of the Knowe, – bought a piece of ground and collected by subscription the sum of £75.5.6 to build a new school with a house for the school master. The school was called the "Subscription School."

The school was situated on the east side of the Goat, half way between Castlebank Street and Dumbarton Road. It was a stone building with an outside stair leading to the schoolhouse above the schoolroom. The school was a typical village school where all the children sat side by side regardless of the social standing of their parents.

Throughout its existence, the school was most successful and the standard of education was high. Apart from the latter days, the roll was never below one hundred pupils. The demise of the school was due to the competition from the church schools, particularly the Partick Parish Church School adjoining the church and the Free Church School in Anderson Street. After the school was closed, the building was used for many years as the workshop of a local joiner.

Between 1825 and 1830 a school for younger children was held in Castlebank Street in a thatched cottage opposite the weaving factory. This school was known as Dr Neil's school.

Anderson Street School

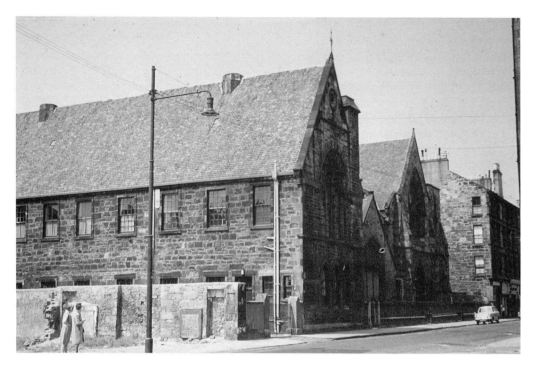

The Anderson Street School is the oldest remaining school building in Partick and was built by the Free Church in 1846.

The Free Church was formed in 1843 – the year of the Disruption. The Disruption was a serious schism in the Church of Scotland when about one third of the ministers and elders walked out of the General Assembly in Edinburgh. The reason for their action was their unwillingness to submit to what they considered the state control of the Church.

The Free Church felt it was its duty to establish a school connected to each church. The Partick Free Church School was founded in 1846 as a School of Industry for Girls where they received a basic education along with instruction in simple domestic arts particularly needlecraft. The original building was single storied but in 1850 it was extended westwards and became a mixed school.

In 1858, it was discovered there were about 400 children who were not attending school, as their parents could not afford even the two-pence per week, the lowest fee charged in the Subscription School. The Mission in the Goat was not fully used and it was decided to use it as a Public School, for the poorest in the town. One of the clauses in the Constitution of the Mission School was that " the fee to be charged should not exceed One Penny per week."

As a result the Mission School became known as the "Penny a week school."

Tom Burns wrote in his Clydeside Musings published in 1912;

The "Penny a week" that guid auld schule,
a name now seldom heard,
The "Burgey Raw", whawr lasses braw,
an strappin chiels were reared,
Auld "Wallace Place" an "Lawrie's Kirk"
an "Peetry's" Bakehoose roon,
Ha'e vanished wi' the march o' time
frae dear auld Partick toon.

The Education Act (Scotland) 1872 completely re-organised education in Scottish schools. Before this Act, education was mainly provided by the church. The Act established School Boards to organise and control education within each parish, and to build new schools where required. Education in Partick came under the control of the Govan School Board.

In 1874, Partick Free Church transferred its school to the new School Board. In 1875, the building was enlarged and a second storey added. It became Anderson Street Public School and was used as an ordinary primary school until Stewartville School was opened in 1891. Since then, it has continued to be used for educational purposes. It has been in turn a centre for woodwork instruction, an overflow for Roscvale Street School and a "dinner school" for local children. In 1940, it became a nursery school.

Stewartville Primary

Stewartville Primary School was built by the Govan School Board. It was opened by Mr J. Parker Smith of Jordanhill, the local Member of Parliament. The site cost £3,347 and the construction and equipment costs added up to £16,620. It had accommodation for 1,500 pupils. In the basement, there was a swimming pond, which was a feature of most of the schools built by the Govan School Board. In 1930, Stewartville School became St. Peter's (Boys) Primary School. St. Peter's transferred to Chancellor Street in 1981.

"Stewartville" is the name applied to a housing development of 46 flats in the former Stewartville Primary School.

Partick Academy

In the middle of the last century, Partick was an expanding community and while there was provision for basic education, a need arose for a higher level of education. In 1848, five local businessmen formed a company and had a private school built – Partick Academy.   Ground was purchased in Church Street and a substantial building erected.

A highly qualified staff was selected and a wide range of subjects was offered. Apart from the academic subjects of English, History, Geography, Mathematics, Modern Languages and Classics provision was also made for Writing and Bookkeeping, Music, Dancing and Deportment, Art, Fencing and Gymnastics.

The building in Church Street was sold to the Govan School Board in 1873 and became the site of Church Street School.

A new building shown below was erected in Peel Street, and opened in 1878.

Due to serious competition, the school suffered a decrease in the intake of pupils, which forced its closure in 1885.

This competition came from the high quality Higher Grade Schools of the Govan School Board and in particular from the nearby Hamilton Crescent Higher Grade School. More competition came from the boys schools of Glasgow Academy, which had moved westwards, and the opening of Kelvinside Academy. In addition, the girls schools of Westbourne, Laurel Bank and Park were founded at this time.

After the building closed it was known for a number of years as the Assembly Rooms where all kinds of social events were held. In 1918 it was purchased by the YMCA and was run under its auspices as the Western Institute.

During the Second World War Hyndland School used the building as a canteen. For a time the building lay unoccupied and was sold to developers. However, the building fell into disrepair and the costs of renovation became prohibitive. The building was demolished and the site which is still derelict is beside the Hanover Crescent sheltered housing development.

Hamilton Crescent School

By the 1880s, basic education was provided at primary school level but higher education was only for children whose parents could afford to pay fees. These children attended the grammar school or the academy where most of the places were either endowment or fee-paying.

The Govan School Board realised the need for a secondary school in Partick and decided to start building on a site in Hamilton Crescent. The school was opened on 27th May 1887 with Mr John Lunn, a former rector of Partick Academy, as its first Head Master. It was a fee-paying school with some free places for children of parents with more modest incomes. The education was of a very high standard, mainly academic, with preparation for university a prime concern. The school was proud of its local roots and incorporated the motto of the burgh "Industria Ditat" in its badge.

By the early twentieth century, the school roll had increased so much that in 1908 three classes had to be accommodated in the former Partick Manse, which had become part of the Middlefield Special School. A site for a new school was sought and the School Board decided on one in Clarence Drive.

In its early years, Hamilton Crescent School provided predominantly academic subjects but later this was extended to include technical and commercial subjects. The commercial subjects were particularly popular and many girls opted for Hamilton Crescent School instead of Hyndland because they wanted to pursue a business career. However in April 1912 there was an exodus of staff and pupils to Hyndland School leaving Hamilton Crescent to fulfil the role of a junior secondary.

In 1972 Hamilton Crescent School was closed and the pupils transferred to Hyndland Secondary while Hyndland Primary was closed and the pupils from that school were transferred to the Hamilton Crescent building.

Hyndland School – "The Old Building"

Hyndland School was opened on 11th February 1912 and was known as Hyndland Higher Grade School. It was built in Locharbiggs sandstone in the "Renaissance Style" at a cost of £25,159 and provided accommodation for 1,100 secondary pupils and 300 primary pupils.

In contrast to its classical style, the building contained well-equipped physics and chemistry laboratories and an art room. The heating system was the "Plenum System" where hot air passed through ducts in the building. One difficulty with this system was, that if a room became overheated or stuffy the opening of a window interrupted the flow of hot air and the neighbouring room would cool rapidly. The school was fully lit by electricity, which in 1912 was something of an innovation because the most common illuminant for houses and public buildings was gas.

While the primary department catered mainly for local children, the secondary department had pupils from a much wider area, including Jordanhill and Scotstoun. The emphasis was very much on academic subjects and although there was a small woodwork department, the school offered no commercial subjects.

Until the 1920s pupils could sit the Intermediate Examination in Third year and as this certificate was accepted as entry to a large number of professions, including medicine, quite a number of pupils left in Third Year. Those who continued were generally studying for university entrance. The pupils who were interested in pursuing a teaching career without a university qualification had to transfer in their Fifth Year to Hillhead High School to take the "Junior Student Course" for entry to teacher training college.

It became clear in the mid 1920s that the school could not cope with the intake from its feeder schools and it was necessary to have over-spill classes in Dowanhill and Church Street Schools. Fortunately, there was sufficient land adjacent to build the additional space required and the "New Building" was opened in 1930.

The "Old Building" is now known as the "Airlie Building."

Hyndland School – The "New Building"

The much needed extension to Hyndland School – now called the "Lauderdale Building" – was opened in August 1930 by Sir Thomas Kelly, the Lord Provost of Glasgow. The New Building had room for 800 additional pupils bringing the capacity of the school up to about 2,000. One of the innovations was a fully furnished flat for domestic science teaching. In addition, as the headmaster, Walter Jamieson, was a wireless pioneer he had loud speakers erected in the playground over which at morning intervals intimations could be made. Later a broadcast system was installed and every room had a speaker. This system was used for a variety of purposes such as sports reports, quiz games and general announcements. It was the first such system to be used in a Scottish school and was copied in other schools.

In 1972 the school merged with Hamilton Crescent and became fully comprehensive. Five years later the Old Building was gutted by fire. The refurbishment was completed in 1981 with the addition of a computer lab and a lecture hall.

The Anderson College of Medicine

The Anderson College is adjacent to the Western Infirmary on Dumbarton Road. It was the last building designed by the Glasgow architect James Sillers and was completed by John Keppie in 1889. In the semi-circular recess above the window, there is a sculpture by Pittendrigh Macgillivray, which features an operation. It closed down as a medical school in 1948 and now houses the Molecular Genetics department of Glasgow University.

The original Anderson College was on the north side of Bath Street just east of Renfield Street. Many Scottish doctors of an earlier day were trained in the Anderson College. The training for the Licentiate of the Royal College of Physicians and Surgeons could be undertaken there. It was the college where David Livingstone received his medical training.

The Punda Tree

This case contains a cross section of a branch of the Punda Tree under which David Livingstone heart was buried in what is now Zimbabwe. For many years, the case was fixed to the wall of the entrance hall to the Anderson College. It is now in the Hunterian museum.

Father Daniel Gallagher who was the Parish Priest at St Peter's in Partick from 1855-1883 was a boyhood companion of David Livingstone and they remained friends through out their lives. As young boys, they both worked in the cotton mill in Blantyre and Gallagher tutored Livingstone in classical education.

Religion

Partick Churches

In 1769, the people of Partick made an appeal to the Parish Church of Govan to provide a church on the north bank of the River Clyde. At that time, churchgoers in Partick had either to cross the River Clyde by ferry to worship in Govan Parish Church, or travel three miles to the church in Anderston.

Normally the first church in a growing community was the Parish Church, however, Partick was a weaving community and most Scottish weavers were Radicals and so were sympathetic to the breakaway denominations. The first organised religious services in Partick were held in the 1820s in Dr Neil's School in Castlebank Street. The numbers attending these services steadily increased and a petition for the erection of a church was presented to the Secession and Relief Presbyteries of Glasgow. The Secession group were the first to be granted a site and in 1824 their church was completed at the corner of Byres Road and Dumbarton Road. A few months later the Relief Congregation built a church on the site of the present day Partick South Church in Dumbarton Road. The church prospered and a new building was opened in 1864. In 1867 it became Newton Place United Presbyterian Church.

It was not until 1834 that the Parish Church was built on a piece of spare ground to the west of the quarry, now known as Church Street. Around 1860 some residents felt that it was desirable that an Established Church should be erected in the western part of Partick to meet the need of the rapidly increasing population in that area. In 1865 St Mary's was built in Peel Street. At the end of the nineteenth century, with a further increase in population, Govan Parish Church sponsored the building of the beautiful St Brides Church in Rosevale Street.

The Disruption of 1843 had many supporters in Partick, those in sympathy formed a congregation, and in 1844, the Partick Free Church was built. In 1900 the church shown below became known as Anderson United Free Church, after its founder minister Henry Anderson.

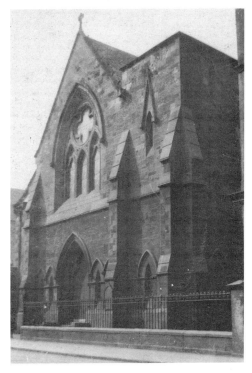

In the middle of last century, church going was a practice of the well to do. Partick United Free High Church was formed to create additional space for the district's poor to worship. It was originally, a wooden "shed," in Orchard (Vine) Street then a wooden church in Merkland Street. In 1869 it moved to Partick High in Hamilton Crescent. Other U.F. churches formed were the Victoria Park U. F. Church, which opened a new building in Balshagray Avenue in 1877 and Dowanvale

U. F. Church which was built in 1880 at the intersection of Clarendon and Dowanhill Streets. Partick High and Dowanvale united in 1936.

At the beginning of the nineteenth century, Partick was overwhelmingly Protestant. James Napier noted that there was only one Roman Catholic in the district in 1820. However, this was to change during the 1840s and 1850s with the Irish diaspora in the wake of the famine of the late 1840s. After an initial phase of a Catholic mission led by Father Gallagher, St. Peter's Church, in Bridge Street, was consecrated in May 1858. The church was closed in 1903 when St Peter's was opened in Hyndland Street. Due to pressure of numbers, the Bridge Street building was reopened in 1923. In 1945, it became the separate parish of St Simon's. Today the Polish Community in Glasgow worship in St Simon's shown in the photograph below.

The Partick Society of Methodists was formed in 1869 and their church in Dumbarton Road was opened in 1882. At the same time, the Congregationalists built a church in Stewartville Street and later the Baptists built one at the foot of Crow Road. Next to the garage in Hayburn Street was a little church, the daughter church of St Silas Episcopal Church in Woodside.

In 1881, the Partick Temple Corps of the Salvation Army started in Vine Street, and after a number of moves the present Temple in Peel Street was opened in 1956. The Christian Brethren worship in the Abingdon Halls in Stewartville Street.

The increasing number of West Highland inhabitants was also catered for. Gardner Street Church was started in 1875 as a mission for Gaelic speakers, the present building being erected in 1898. At the foot of Crow Road is Partick Free Church. The congregation is mainly of Highland extraction and uses the Gaelic language in their services. Another such church is Partick Highland Free Church, which occupies the original Dowanvale Church.

Religion played a very important part in life in the community during the latter part of the nineteenth and the first half of the twentieth centuries. However, in the latter part of the twentieth century, church attendance fell away and many of the churches, which had once seen large congregations on a regular basis, were now being attended by ever fewer people.

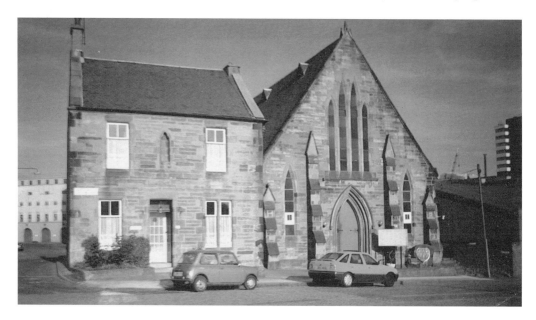

Churches that faced this all too typical situation were Newton Place, Partick Anderson, and Hamilton Crescent. Hamilton Crescent was already the result of an amalgamation of St. Mary's, Partick High, and Dowanvale. Together, Newton Place, Partick Anderson, and Hamilton Crescent were amalgamated in 1978 to form Partick South Church. The new congregation occupied the former Newton Place Church on Dumbarton Road. This building was demolished in 1983 and a new building was dedicated on April 19th 1988.

The Dowanhill and Partick East congregations merged and united in the Partick East building. A few years later Old Partick Parish in Church Street closed and its congregation united with Partick East to form Partick Trinity Church. Dowanhill church was sold in 1984 for the nominal sum of £1 to the Four Acres Charitable Trust and is now the Cottier Theatre Project named after Daniel Cottier who hand-painted the interior of the church.

The Quakers' Burial Ground

This burial ground is on the west side of Keith Street. The ground itself is a small plot of land surrounded by a stone wall and fronted with ornate railings.

In the eighteenth and nineteenth centuries Quakers faced severe discrimination throughout Britain and were banned from burying their dead in ordinary churchyards. In 1711, John Purdon, a local landowner who was married to a Quaker, gifted the plot of land to the Society of Friends.

Quaker funerals in the village were far from respectfully solemn occasions in the nineteenth century. The locals, and in particular youths, would crowd around the walls and jeer and heckle the mourners. This was one of the reasons why burials were abandoned in the graveyard in 1857.

The Society of Friends gave the burial ground to the Commissioners of Partick in perpetuity on the condition that the ground be kept in order and that a shilling be paid annually to the Society of Friends. The plate on the gate was prised off a number of years ago and was rescued as it was about to be put in a foundry. It was restored and is now firmly attached to the back wall.

Entertainment

The Star Palace – F & F Bingo Hall

In 1881 two large engineering shops were built in Partick on the south side of Dumbarton Road about 300 yards east of Partick Cross for William Smith and Sons who specialised in making boilers, milling equipment and weighing machines. The building nearest the Cross was demolished some years ago, the other building became, in 1911, a music hall known as the Star Palace.

The Star Palace was a very successful provincial music hall and, like similar provincial music halls such as the Lyceum in Govan, it attracted many noted productions and artists of the day. Amongst the artists who performed were Durward Lely, the original Nanki-poo, McKenzie Murdoch, the violinist who was also known as the Scottish Paganini, R.C.Hamilton, tenor, and Dr Walford Bodie, the illusionist. At Christmas a pantomime was produced and from time to time "Go as you Please" competitions were held.

The Star Palace was a casualty of the economic downturn after the First World War and was closed in 1927. For a short time afterwards it operated as a cinema but was bought over by Fyfe and Fyfe Limited and became a dance hall. After a few years it became a roller skating rink and in 1961, when bingo, along with other forms of gambling, became legal it became a bingo hall.

The Partick Star Palace is oftened confused with the Glasgow Star Palace where, in 1884, fourteen people were trampled to death when a false cry of "Fire" caused a stampede.

Other places of entertainment in Partick were the Partick Picture House in Vine Street, the Western Cinema (the Garrick), the Standard Picture House, the Rosevale, and the Tivoli in Crow Road.

Sport

Partick Curling Club

The Partick Curling Club was formed in 1842, in Burns Cottage on the site of the Glasgow University Lodge in Dumbarton Road. The curling club is the oldest club in Partick. For the first six years, it is not clear, where the curling took place. However, in 1848, ground was leased on the west side of Byres Road opposite Great George Street.

The pond on this ground became known as Clayholes Curling Pond. It can be assumed that the Curlers Pub in Byres Road acquired the name by its close proximity to the pond. This building can be recognised on the 1842 map as the only house on Byres Road north of the junction with Church Street. In 1856, the ground at Clayholes was required for quarrying and the club had to find a site for a new pond. Ground was subsequently obtained in Peel Street adjoining the Partick Bowling Club, which had been formed in 1844.

The Curling Club was not able to stay at that site long and was forced to move when the land was required for building. This time they moved to a pond called Craft Crown situated at the west end of Queensborough Gardens close to the railway. The club remained there until 1894.

In 1893, the club approached the Burgh of Partick for the lease of ground in Victoria Park for the construction of a curling pond and a strip of ground bordering Balshagray Avenue was obtained. Provost Wood opened the new pond on January 8th 1894.

In 1899, two brothers M. Hunter Kennedy and John Kennedy offered to construct two rinks in Victoria Park and another brother Baillie (later Provost) William Kennedy offered to build a clubhouse. Both offers were accepted and the rinks and the Clubhouse were opened in 1902.

For many years, the curling was carried out at Crossmyloof Ice Rink until it closed in December 1985. The Summit Centre Ice Rink in Minerva Way, Finnieston opened in February 1986 and was used by Partick Curling Club. When the Summit Centre closed in March 1998 the club moved to the Waterfront Complex in Greenock .

The Partick Funeral Bell was fixed to a stand and the Curling Club held an annual competition for the trophy, starting in 1859. If a member, who lived outside the Burgh boundary, won the competition, he could not take possession of the Bell since it could not leave the Burgh.

Hamilton Crescent Cricket Ground

The West of Scotland Cricket Club was formed at Hamilton Crescent in 1862 and has played there ever since. Prior to its formation, two clubs played there, Clutha in the northern part and the Royal in the southern. The players of Clutha, with some Glasgow businessmen, were responsible for the creation of the new club. One of the businessmen, Colonel (later Sir) David Buchanan became president. He was devoted to cricket and gave considerable financial support to the club.

Hamilton Crescent housed many sporting activities other than cricket. From the 1870s until 1939, the cricket club shared the ground with the West of Scotland Rugby Club. The playing pitch bordered Burgh Hall Street where there was a small covered stand. This stand was damaged in the air raid of March 1942 and had to be demolished. After the Second World War the rugby club did not resume playing at Hamilton Crescent

In the early 1900s, four rugby internationals were played and in 1914 a Hockey international.

The first three soccer internationals between Scotland and England were also held in this ground – the first one in 1872 was a draw; Scotland won the other two. The Scottish Cup Final of 1876-1877 took place there when the Vale of Leven beat Glasgow Rangers by 3 goals to 2.

The Thomlinson "T" Football

The Thomlinson "T" Football was a celebrated product of Partick and was used by football teams throughout the world. It was made in the saddlery workshop of William Thomlinson in Norval Street at the foot of Crow Road.

The panelling comprised of the ingenious interlacing of pieces of leather each in the form of a letter "T." The panelling was slightly altered later to produce what was known as the Improved "T" which is shown in the photograph and subsequently modified again to become the Gold "T."

William Thomlinson started his saddlers business in a small way in 1876 producing mainly horse harness and leather equipment for local farmers. Around 1890, he formed the Greenbank Leather Works with a shop at 450 Dumbarton Road and shared the premises with his brother John Thomlinson who ran a printing business. His brother John produced the illustration shown. In addition, William had a tannery in Maryhill where the hides were prepared for the factory.

As time went on, Thomlinson diversified into making other sports equipment such as golf bags, cricket, hockey and golf balls. Subsequently the production of golf equipment surpassed that of footballs. At peak production, about 120 workers were employed.

In 1908, the firm moved to a new six-storey building behind the saddlers' shop, which had access to Norval Street. The firm stayed in this location until its closure in 1983. The building was then converted into flats.

KICKED ALL OVER THE GLOBE

IMPROVED

This is a specimen of THOMLINSON'S NEW ONE-PIECE SHOWCARD (Patent Pending) DESIGNED AND PRODUCED BY JOHN THOMLINSON LIMITED STANLEY WORKS, GLASGOW W.I

The many advantages of this new type Showcard are listed on the back

His brother's business started in 1874 when he took over a small print works. Around 1890, he established the Stanley Works in Norval Street at the foot of Crow Road. Additions were made in 1896, 1904, and 1908. In 1909, the printing firm was incorporated as a limited firm of printers, carton makers, and envelope makers. For many years, an important product was the "Bontuk" envelope, an early easy sealing envelope. The firm which still specialises in printing and carton making, moved to modern premises in Clydebank in 1996.

Partick Thistle

Meadowside Park

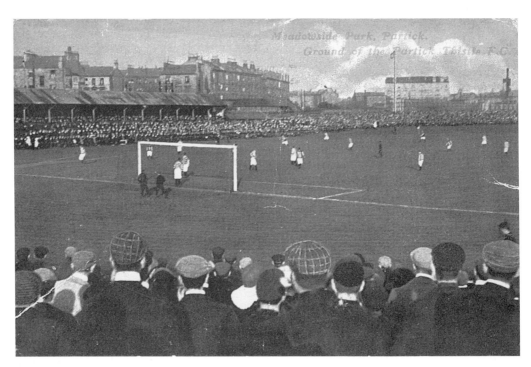

Meadowside Park was the home of Partick Thistle from 1887 until 1908. It had a capacity of 20,000 and stand seating for 900. The pitch bordered the Clyde and occasionally the ball ended up in the river. During games, a rowing boat with two men was on duty to retrieve the ball. Thistle had to leave in 1908, as the ground was required for the construction of the Meadowside Quay. Without a pitch, Thistle accepted an offer from Rangers to share Ibrox for the 1908-1909 season.

The development of Partick Thistle from amateur to professional was as follows:

1876   Partick Thistle was formed and their first recorded game was on 23rd October 1877 against Huntingdon on the site of the present Art Galleries. Thistle won this game 4-1

1881   Jordanvale Park was leased near the present day entrance to the Clyde Tunnel. This was their home for three years.

1883   Thistle moved to Muirpark on the west side of Gardner Street bordering Dumbarton Road.

1885   The next ground was Inchview Park, almost opposite Balshagray Avenue. This had been the ground of the recently defunct Partick Football Club.

1887   Thistle took occupancy of Meadowside Park.

1909   Firhill became the home of Partick Thistle. They rented it for six years from the Caledonian Railway Company and bought it in 1916 for £5,500.

The Scottish Cup

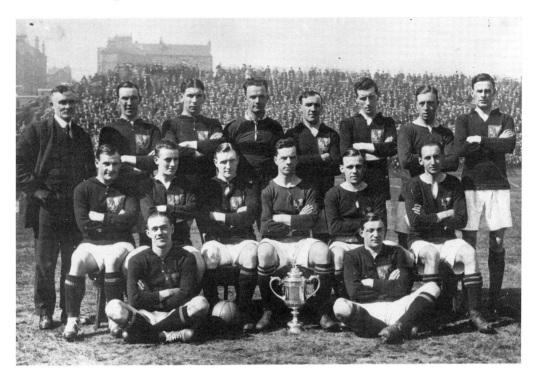

Two of the greatest upsets that Partick Thistle (The Great Unpredictables) inflicted were on the 16th April 1921 and 23rd October 1971.

On 16th April 1921, Partick Thistle beat Glasgow Rangers 1-0 in the final of the Scottish Cup at Celtic Park in front of a crowd of only 28,000 since there was a boycott against a recent doubling of ticket prices – the previous year's attendance was 95,000. Rangers were by far the favourites and few people gave Thistle any chance especially since Rangers had cruised through the preliminary rounds and Thistle had no fewer than four replays. The team also had a number of injuries. John Blair scored the winning goal.

The Thistle team was: Campbell, Crichton, Bulloch, Harris, M. Wilson, Borthwick, Blair, Kinloch, D. Wilson, McMenemy, and Salisbury, substitute Johnstone

On 23rd October 1971, Thistle beat Celtic in the Final of the Scottish League Cup. On their way to the final, Thistle had a good run of seven unbeaten games. In the Quarter Final they went down 2-0 at St. Johnstone but came back to win 5-1 at home. In the Semi Final, they beat Falkirk 2-0 at Hampden. In the Final against Celtic, Thistle scored four times in the first half with Rae, Lawrie, McQuade, and Bone. Dalglish scored in the second half to make the final score 4-1 to Thistle.

The Thistle team was: Rough, Hansen, Forsyth, Glavin, Campbell, Strachan, McQuade, Coulston, Bone, Rae, and Lawrie, substitute Gibson

Public Parks

Victoria Park

The Partick Municipal Authorities had for many years wanted to provide the people of Partick with a suitable public park and this was mooted officially in 1867. However, it was not until 1885 that negotiations began with James Oswald the owner of Scotstoun Estate which was on the western fringe of the burgh near Whiteinch.

The construction of the park began in 1886 and provided much needed work to the area. The park stretched for about half a mile from east to west and 250 yards from north to south.

The park was named to commemorate Queen Victoria's Jubilee and was opened in great style in July 1887 by Sir Andrew McLean, Provost of Partick. A general holiday was declared and a procession took place from the Burgh Hall comprising the Provost, Magistrates, the local corps of the Lanark Rifle Volunteers, the Police Force, the Fire Brigade, foresters, gardeners, masons and shepherds. There were also employees from the shipyards and works in the neighbourhood.

The gates shown were gifted by the women of Partick who raised the entire cost of £200 by voluntary subscription. The gates in the photograph were in Balshagray Avenue about 200 yards from Dumbarton Road. With the building of an approach road to the Clyde Tunnel the gates were moved and re-erected at the entrance to the park in Victoria Park Drive North. The Whiteinch pond was also affected by the new road. It was originally in the shape of a crown but as the construction work encroached on the park, the shape was altered slightly.

The Fossil Grove

Victoria Park occupies much of the land of Balshagray Farm. To the west of the farm was a small tree covered knoll known locally as the Tinker's Wood, a stopping place for travelling people. This knoll had been quarried for dolerite, a hard igneous rock suitable for road making which had been used in the construction of Dumbarton Road. It was approached by a narrow lane from Dumbarton road along the line of the present Victoria Park Street. When the Victoria Park was being landscaped a cut was made through the wood and some fine examples of fossilised trees were discovered. Fortunately, the Geology Department of Glasgow University was consulted and the excavation was carried out carefully. A building was erected over the fossils to protect them.

It is estimated that the fossilised trees are 250 million years old. The environment that the trees grew in differed greatly from current conditions. It was much warmer and wetter. The trees probably grew in a swampy estuary or lagoon and were killed by the deposition of mud and sand. The stumps then decayed, became hollow and the mud and sand entered right down to the roots. These depositions solidified and formed shale and sandstone so the stumps became casts of hard rock.

Cross Park

This photograph shows the main gate of Cross Park in Crow Road just south of Broomhill Cross. Cross Park was at one time a small private estate around what was known as Cross Mansion. A number of years ago, the stone pillars of the original gateway were replaced by metal gate supports. The house was in private ownership until the First World War when it became a hostel for refugees from Belgium. It came on the market and for a time, it was proposed to be a Model Lodging House. However, Glasgow Corporation bought it and the ground became a public park.

The Recreation Grounds

RECREATION GROUNDS, POLICE DRILL HALL
& GYMNASIUM, HOZIER ST, PARTICK   Nº 488

The ground for this park was purchased in 1895 partly from Sir William Hozier, the local landowner, and partly from the Caledonian Railway Company.

The Partick Burgh Police Force was at that time under the command of Captain Cameron who, in his prime, was a successful competitor at the Highland Games. Captain Cameron persuaded the Commissioners of Partick to build a gymnasium in Hozier (Beith) Street. He encouraged his officers to take part in athletic training and many of them became noted for their prowess at the Highland Games. It is claimed that the Partick Police were at one time World Champions at the Tug o' War.

The gymnasium can be seen at the extreme left of the photograph. It was open to all young men of the burgh and was used for fetes, exhibitions, concerts, and dances. It was burned down many years ago. The Clydeside Expressway was built on the site of the park.

Partick Streets

Old Dumbarton Road

Today Old Dumbarton Road leads from Argyle Street, passes behind the Kelvin Hall, and goes on to the bridge over the Kelvin. This picture shows Dumbarton Road around the middle of last century. For a long time, this was part of the main road from Glasgow to Dumbarton.

The grounds to the left are the policies of Yorkhill House. In the middle right is the Bunhouse Inn – a very old Partick Inn whose original building was erected in 1695. The building shown was built in 1849 and demolished in 1926 to clear ground for the Kelvin Hall. The man at the corner of the building is standing where the goods entrance to the Kelvin Hall is now located.

This photograph shows the junction of Old Dumbarton Road and Argyle Street. The church is St Enoch Church of Scotland. It sustained serious bomb damage during the Second World War and had to be demolished. The site is now occupied by a filling station.

Peel Street

Peel Street, Partick.

The present Peel Street, was formerly a country road which led to Hyndland, known as the Green Loan. It became Rab's Loan and then was finally named Peel Street after Sir Robert Peel who introduced the uniformed police force.

Peel Street at Dumbarton Road became the forum of Partick. Regular weeknight meetings of religious and political groups were held there until the Second World War. On Saturday, there was a succession of meetings starting in the early afternoon. In addition, street entertainers and all sorts of vendors vied for the passer-by's attention. The vendors sold anything from cough cures to an offer to extract teeth.

Willie Ferrie, the Partick Street Minstrel was a well-known entertainer at Peel Street. He always dressed in a tile-hat and frock-coat, bedecked with all kinds of decorations. Willie did actions to his songs, for instance, in "Bonnie Annie Lawrie" he lay down in the gutter – no matter the weather – and "died." He had a pair of bone clappers and would dance round singing a song of his own composition such as;

Willie Ferrie you're a don,
wi the clappers in your haun,
you can play the Rag Time Ban,
Willie you're a champ-i-on

The church on the right was Hamilton Crescent Church of Scotland. The City Temple bought this building and subsequently sold it for the construction of flats.

Part of the terrace opposite the cricket ground was destroyed in the blitz in March 1941 with considerable loss of life. Two men were rescued after being entombed for several days. Although one recovered, the other, a War Reserve Police Constable, died later in hospital.

Gardner Street

Gardner Street, Partick

Gardner Street is the steepest street in Partick and runs from Dumbarton Road to Partickhill Road. On the left is Gardner Street Church of Scotland.

When motor shows came to the Kelvin Hall in the 1920s commercial vehicles used Gardner Street to display their hill climbing ability. Local children tried, often successfully, to outpace the various vehicles, which attempted the hill. Another game was for boys to attempt to cycle up the whole length of Gardner Street. An example of this was a lad called George McDonald, known locally as "Geordie Crome." He was successful in his climb but on the way down he hurtled down Gardner Street and scattered the crowd, which had gathered to watch him.

Dumbarton Road at Hayburn Street

This photograph was taken early this century. Apart from the tramcar, the vehicles are horse-drawn. A trough stands beside the pavement to the left of the picture, where horses could be watered. Workmen repairing the tramlines were a common sight in the early days of the tramway as the lines required constant repair.

The tram depot in Hayburn Street was built in 1894 and extended in 1901. When the tram service was discontinued in Glasgow in 1962, the depot was converted into a bus garage for the Corporation Transport Service. It was later transferred to the Education Department and is now used as a garage.

A War Memorial for the members of Partick Tram Depot who were killed during the First World War was at one time fixed to the wall in Hayburn Street.

The gents' outfitter in the photograph, D.M. Hoey, which opened in 1918, is still operating at the corner of Hayburn Street.

Dumbarton Road at Newton Place Church

The picture above is of Dumbarton Road at Stewartville Street looking westwards. On the left is the wall of Newton Place Church now Partick South Church. West of this wall are two cottages, which were demolished to make way for the building of Partick Library. Dr Kirk and Dr Sutherland who were both well-known doctors in Partick occupied the Cottages.

On the opposite side of the road at the clock were the premises of Messrs Peden, for many years jewellers and watch repairers in Partick. The shop is now part of the offices of Archibald Sharp & Sons, an old established Partick legal firm. The view looking eastwards is shown below.

Balshagray Avenue

Balshagray Avenue Whiteinch.   69274 (IV)

A number of meanings for Balshagray have been suggested. In a well-known glossary of Scottish Place names "the town of the decayed or withered flock" is given from the Gaelic "Baile-seac-graighe" but Gaelic scholars are far from certain about this derivation. A much more probable derivation is from "Baile-sealg-an-rign" or "the town of the hunting of the King" as Balshagray was the name of the area when it was still forest, farming and crofting being a comparatively recent activity.

The Kings of Strathclyde had a castle at the mouth of the River Kelvin and may well have had a hunting lodge in the hilly area to the north of Whiteinch. This is supported by two local place names. There was a short road behind Balshagray School, which was called the Rotten Row. This comes from the Gaelic "Rat-an Rign" – "the Road of the King" and may well have been part of a road leading to the hunting lodge. In addition, at one time there were four farms in the area with the name "balgray." This is a corruption of "Baile-an-Rign" – "Town of the King."

The church on the left of the avenue was Victoria Park Church. This church was compulsorily purchased and demolished when the approaches to the Clyde Tunnel replaced the lower part of Balshagray Avenue.

Partick Tenements

Muirhead Street

Muirhead Street ran between Anderson Street and Purdon Street (formerly Douglas Street) near to Castlebank Street. It is now part of the new roadway and new housing development at the foot of Purdon Street.

During the middle and latter part of last century, Partick was a vibrant and expanding industrial community. It attracted many workers from the rural areas of Scotland, particularly the Highlands and Islands, and from Ireland. The housing for these workers and their families was built mainly to the south of Dumbarton Road. Right up until the 1960s certain streets in Partick still had predominantly either Highland or Irish inhabitants with their distinctive traditions and religions.

Serious overcrowding was common in such houses and the authorities introduced a category termed "Ticketed House" where a small metal plate was attached to the door and indicated the number of person permitted to sleep in the house. Inspectors from the local authorities were authorised to enter the house at night and find if there was overcrowding.

The houses shown here were built in Muirhead Street around 1870. The photograph was taken immediately before their demolition in the mid 1960s. They were mainly room and kitchen houses with a number of single apartments. All had running water and a communal toilet on the stairway.

Gullane Street

These tenements were in Gullane Street, formerly Wilson Street, just off Purdon Street.

The smaller building to the left was built for the Burgh of Partick in the 1880s to provide accommodation for policemen and firemen. The houses were two apartments. The larger building to the right was built of Locharbriggs sandstone at the turn of the century and was of good quality.

Early this century some houses in Wilson Street were rented by a local committee and run as a day nursery for children of working mothers. The close was known locally as the "Nursery Close" and for many years, a Miss Mackenzie was in charge of the nursery. It closed in the 1920s when childcare needs were increasingly being met by the local authority.

The brick construction in front of the building had been a wartime air-raid shelter. To the left of the building is a pend. This is a passage for vehicles to gain access to the back of the building. It was to the back of the building that in 1901 a large three floored brick building was built as the Thistle Cabinet Work of J. Reid and Co. which produced quality furniture. In what is now Purdon Street, practically the whole length of the building on the ground floor was a large showroom for furniture. The firm closed down in the 1930s because of the depression. Subsequently the factory made the "Kismet" razor blade and finally became a store for local furnishers Benzie and Co.

Partick Notables

James B Napier, F.R.S.E., F.C.S.

James Napier, the son of a calico worker, was born in 1810 in a small house at the south-east corner of the Goat. His only formal schooling was at age 8 when he spent eleven months in Dr Neil's school in Castlebank Street.

He started work at age 10 and became a "tearer" in the calico works at a wage of 1/3d per week. Later he became a "drawboy" in a weaver's shop at 1/6d per week. He then worked in the dyeworks of Messrs Gilchrist and Co. at Meadowside where the wage was 3/- per week. After a short while he was so well thought of that his wage went up to 5/-. When the foreman dyer left Napier succeeded him at a wage of 11/-.

His health was poor and he was forced to leave the dyeworks. He obtained employment with a chemical firm Messrs Griffen and Co. of Glasgow. He attended classes in the Andersonian College, now the University of Strathclyde where he specialised in the chemistry of cloth dying and in the new art of electro-plating. In 1842, he was appointed to a leading post with the electro-plating firm of Elkington and Mason in London.

In 1849, he had to return to Partick due to ill health and he set up as a consultant chemist. He showed great interest in the health of the people of Partick and proved that the disposal of sewage and the supply of domestic water were serious health hazards.

It was acknowledged that the best way to affect change was to have Partick constituted as a Police Burgh. This was done at a meeting called by the Sheriff in the Free Church School on 17th June 1852.

Mr Napier was highly regarded as a historian of Partick and his book *Notes and Reminiscences relating to Partick*, published in 1873 contains a wealth of information on the early days of the village.

Big Rachael

The "Owl"

Big Rachael – Mrs Rachael Hamilton or Johnston was a well-known Partick worthy during the latter part of the nineteenth century. She originally came from Northern Ireland, was 6 ft 4 inches tall and weighed between 16 and 17 stones. All her life she engaged in strenuous work. She was a general labourer with Tod, McGregor's, the Shipbuilders in Meadowside, and she also worked in the Anchor Line Sheds. For a time, she worked as a forewoman navvy at the Jordanhill Brickworks and latterly she was a farm worker in Mr Simpson's farm at Anniesland. During the Partick Riots of the 1870s, she served as a Special Constable

William McDougall – the "Owl" was the owner and editor of the *Western News* a popular Partick weekly paper, which he founded in 1891.

He wrote under the pen name of the "Owl." The name was inspired by an owl, which nested in a cave in Victoria Park. This owl could see the world go by in the park and gave Mr McDougall the idea that the "Owl" would be a suitable name for someone reporting the happenings within the community.

His "Notes by the Owl" were well known for searing attacks on hypocrisy and for caustic comments on local events. The "Owl" was critical of those found guilty in the local court giving lurid details of their misdemeanours. At the same time, he could be just as critical of the Bench. It was said that those found guilty were more frightened of the publicity of the "Owl" than the decision of the court.

The paper remained in his control until his death in 1944. His son, who was very politically motivated, renamed it *The Western Pioneer News* with the purpose "to pioneer a new social order." The paper ceased publication in 1950.

Baillie Izett

John Izett was a man of adventure. For 13 years, he was the stores manager of the Rio Tinto Company in Huelva in Spain. He then opened a draper's shop in Glasgow, but after seven years, decided to try his luck prospecting in East Africa. On his return, he opened a draper's business on the south side of Dumbarton Road almost opposite Crow Road.

The early years of this century were a very emotive time for the people of Partick. There were those who supported the annexation of the Burgh of Partick into the City of Glasgow and those who were opposed. Mr Izett supported the annexation and in 1911 he stood for the Partick Council but was defeated. However, in 1912, after the annexation he stood for the Partick West Ward of the Glasgow Town Council and was elected. In 1918, he unsuccessfully stood against Sir Robert Horne as Member of Parliament for Hillhead. He became senior Magistrate of the City of Glasgow in 1922.

James Neil Reid

James Neil Reid was a highly respected personality in Partick at the turn of the century. For many years he carried on a successful business as a retail and wholesale confectioner at 226, Dumbarton Road, just to the east of Hyndland Street.

Early in his life, he became a member of the Salvation Army and for 28 years, he was Sergeant Major of the Partick Corps. He was particularly active amongst the needy at a time when help for the poor was very meagre. He gave food to people in distress, provided accommodation at night shelters for down and outs, and obtained medicine for the sick. Every Sunday morning he went round the cells in the Partick Police Office to give comfort and advice to the drunks who had been arrested on the Saturday night.

In 1922 he stood for the Town Council as an Independent and came out top of the poll. He was known as the "Poor People's Councillor". He died in 1923 and the funeral from his home in Peel Street was one of the largest ever seen in Partick. It was estimated that 15,000 people turned out. People lined Peel Street and along a good part of Dumbarton Road.

Before and after Redevelopment

Dumbarton Road eastwards from Hyndland Street

Dumbarton Road at Rosevale Street

Dumbarton Road with Broomhill Drive on the left

Broomhill Drive looking on to Dumbarton Road

Dumbarton Road at Summerfield Cottages

Dumbarton Road at Inchlee Street

The north side of Dumbarton Road east of Haldane Street

The Passing of the Burgh of Partick, 4th November 1912

Writing in 1857 Dr Strang in "Glasgow and its Clubs" says: "At this hour, the landscape painter's occupation about Partick is gone. The village is now a town; it is stretching out on every side, and for some time, it has been shaking hands with Glasgow, as far as gas and lampposts are concerned. Its future destiny will doubtless to be swallowed up like its suburban relatives, Calton, Bridgeton, Gorbals, and Anderston, by an all absorbing parent City."

The fate anticipated by Dr Strang has overtaken the "Balmoral of the Kings of Strathclyde." At midnight on the first Monday of November 1912, the Burgh of Partick ceased to exist. While the Burgh organist played "Lochaber no More" the Provost's chain of office was removed from his neck, and as his robe was laid aside the Provost said, "There they lie, the abandoned habits of the Provost of Partick, taken from him by an Act of Parliament."

Sic transit gloria villae regiae quae Pertnech nuncupatur
(So passes the glory of the Royal Town which is called Partick)

The above is an extract from William Greenhorne's "History of Partick" published in 1928.